JUN   2008

FAQ

TEEN LIFE™

FREQUENTLY ASKED QUESTIONS ABOUT

Puberty

Ann Byers

ROSEN
PUBLISHING®

New York

To Andrew, Cooper, Brent, Tyler, Bethany, Dana, Kevin, and Susan, the first young students to explore this topic with me

Published in 2007 by The Rosen Publishing Group, Inc.
29 East 21st Street, New York, NY 10010

Library of Congress Cataloging-in-Publication Data

Byers, Ann.
Frequently asked questions about puberty / By Ann Byers.
— 1st ed.
p. cm. — (FAQ: teen life)
Includes bibliographical references.
ISBN-13: 978-1-4042-0966-4
ISBN-10: 1-4042-0966-2 (library binding)
1. Puberty—Juvenile literature. I. Title.
QP84.4.B94 2007
612.6'61—dc22

2006018921

Manufactured in the United States of America

Contents

Introduction

Talk to any young person who is going to a new junior high school. Ask what he or she is most concerned about. Nine out of ten will say, "Gym class."

Is it basketball or soccer that worries these preteens? Is it meeting new people? Is it having the right gym clothes? No. These may be minor issues for some, but the overwhelming concern of those entering junior high is something far more basic. It is the shower.

For many eleven- or twelve-year-olds, the school shower represents their greatest fears of adolescence. It exposes their bare bodies with all their new growths or nongrowths. It reveals how they are like—or not like—everyone else. They think it will be a place of stares and snickers. For most, however, the shower does not turn out to be the embarrassing experience they dread.

The middle school years don't have to be an uncomfortable time. They are a time of great change, but change shouldn't scare you. The developments your body will go through are good. When you know what is happening to you, you won't be as worried. Sometimes, when you understand that others are experiencing the same things, you can relax. Knowing and understanding what is going on can take away the anxiety. That is why this book was written: so you will know what to expect and why it is happening to you.

Middle school and high school students are changing, physically, mentally, and socially, from children to adults. They sometimes look and act like adults, and sometimes they look and act like children.

The preteen and early teen years are a bridge between two worlds: the world of childhood and the world of adulthood. Bridges are often a little shaky, and sometimes they are scary. But this one is short, and it leads to a wonderful place.

WHEN AND WHY DOES MY BODY CHANGE?

Think of your life as a journey with stops in different places. Your adventure on Earth begins in your mother's womb. The next stop is infancy. Then come the land of toddlers, the world of children, young adulthood, middle age, and old age. Between childhood and adulthood is a fascinating place called adolescence. It begins with puberty.

What Happens During Puberty?

Adolescence is the period of time when you are becoming an adult. During this time, everything changes. The way you look, the way you think, the way you feel—they all change. Puberty is the time at the beginning of adolescence when your body changes from that of a child to that of a man or woman.

If you were to take two babies—a boy and a girl—and dress them alike and cut their hair the same, you probably

Male and female babies look alike, sound alike, and are equally strong. The differences between boys and girls are not very great until puberty.

could not tell the boy from the girl. This is because the main difference between the two is in their primary sex characteristics. That means that the only difference you can see is that the boy has a penis and the girl has a vagina. When the babies grow up and become adults, you can tell which is which without looking under their clothes. Their body shapes are different. As adults, they have secondary sex characteristics. For females, this means that their breasts have developed and their bodies have become curvy. Males have grown facial and body hair, and their bodies have become muscular. For both, sex organs inside their bodies have developed. The secondary sex characteristics are what give men and women the ability to reproduce, or to have children. Everyone, children included, has primary sex characteristics; adults have secondary sex characteristics. This transformation takes place during puberty.

Developing the ability to reproduce is only part of what happens during puberty. The changes that take place during this time affect nearly every part of your body. Your bones get longer and heavier: girls grow 2 to 8 inches (5 to 20 centimeters), and boys grow 4 to 12 inches (10 to 30 cm). Your muscles become stronger, and the fat in your body is distributed differently. Boys' shoulders get wider, and their hips get narrower; girls' hips get wider, and their waists get narrower. Your skin and hair become oilier. You grow hair in new places. Your voice changes. All your emotions are intensified. Even the way you think is different. During puberty, more changes take place in your body in a shorter time than in almost any other period in your life.

What Makes the Changes Happen?

These changes begin in a very small organ in the brain called the pituitary gland. Only about the size of a pea, this organ is the "master gland." Through hormones, the pituitary gland controls many processes that go on in the body.

Hormones are chemicals that make different parts of the body work. They are made in one organ and sent through the bloodstream to other organs. Each organ has a specific job to do. When the hormones get to their destination, they instruct the

The hypothalamus and pituitary gland release the hormones that begin the processes of puberty. "Hormone" comes from the Greek *hormao*, which means "I excite." A hormone excites, or stimulates, glands to do a specific task.

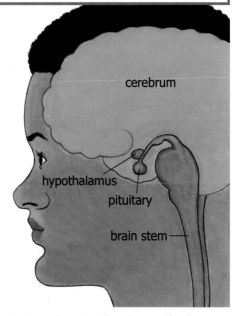

organ to start or stop doing its job. The pituitary gland makes many of the body's hormones, including the hormones that control how a person grows and develops.

Just above the pituitary gland in the brain is the hypothalamus. This is the "command center" that tells many of the organs when to release their hormones. When the time is right for a person to start puberty, the hypothalamus sends the pituitary gland a hormone that says, "Start working." Then the pituitary gland sends different hormones to different body parts that say, "Wake up. It's time to change."

It is not understood how the hypothalamus and the pituitary gland "know" the right time to start the process. The hypothalamus is like a timer in the brain that was set before you were born. The hormones manufactured in the pituitary gland are programmed to release automatically when the timer goes off. Each of us was made with our own individual timer. At just the right moment, the timer goes off, setting everything else in motion.

10 FACTS ABOUT PUBERTY

1 Boys begin puberty about two years later than girls.

2 One in every seven Caucasian American girls starts puberty by age eight; among African American girls, the ratio is nearly one out of every two.

3 During puberty, boys and girls gain about the same amount of weight. Boys gain more muscle, and girls gain more fat.

4 A boy can grow as much as 4 inches (10 cm) in one year during puberty.

5 A person's hands and feet grow before the rest of his or her body during puberty.

6 Boys' muscles nearly double during puberty.

7 All women have about the same amount of breast tissue.

8 Fat gives females their curvy, feminine shape.

9 Mood swings are not just "in your head." They have a biological basis.

10 Although you grow throughout puberty, you grow the fastest during the middle of the two- to six-year span of puberty.

When Do These Changes Happen?

Most people think of adolescence as roughly the teen years. Although the entire period of adolescence usually lasts through most of the teen years, puberty, the beginning of that period, generally occurs somewhat sooner. It can start as early as age eight or as late as sixteen. Girls enter puberty about two years before boys. In North America, girls usually start at twelve, and boys usually start at fourteen.

All the changes do not take place at once. Puberty is a flexible period, meaning it can take as little as a year and a half or as long as six years to complete. We usually consider puberty starting when we see the first signs of physical change. For girls, that is when breasts begin to develop. For boys, it is when the testes and penis start to grow. The end of puberty is usually marked as the time when people reach their adult height. This entire period takes about five years for most girls and six years for most boys.

At the beginning, the changes happen very quickly. It can seem as though your body has suddenly gone crazy. After the first couple of years, things slow down a bit, but you are still changing rapidly. Going from being a child to an adult is a giant step, and to get there, many changes have to take place in a fairly short time.

A few people begin puberty extra early, and a few begin unusually late. Starting puberty before age eight for girls or age nine for boys is called precocious puberty. Starting after age sixteen for girls or fourteen for boys is called delayed puberty. In rare cases, a medical condition can cause precocious or delayed puberty. In those instances, the condition can be treated and development can be put back on track. Most of the time, however, even a very early or a very late puberty does not mean that anything is wrong. Both are simply variations.

Some preteens become embarrassed if they start to develop before their friends do. Others worry when they have not started by the time others have. Sometimes, unkind people tease early or late bloomers or make comments about how they look. If this happens to you, remember that you may be a little ahead of your classmates or a little behind, but you are perfectly normal. Before long, everyone catches up. Each of us has our own internal timer. Your timer might just be a little faster or slower than others'.

When you start puberty depends on a number of factors. The most important is what happened with your parents. If a boy's father developed early, he probably will, too. If a girl's mother started late, she most likely will also start late.

During puberty, your body has extra nutritional needs. Calcium makes your growing bones strong. Protein helps your muscles develop properly, and iron helps energize your new muscle cells.

Diet and health do not seem to affect the timing of puberty for boys, but they do matter for girls. Eating good foods makes the body function best, and poor eating can make puberty start early or late. Girls who are overweight due to an unhealthful diet often begin puberty early because fat causes hormones to be produced. If you do not have enough protein and calcium in your diet, puberty could be delayed. Exercising too much can also postpone development.

For as long as we know, boys have generally experienced puberty between the ages of eleven and seventeen. Girls,

Exercising may do more to build bones than getting calcium from your food. During adolescence, you need at least twenty minutes of vigorous exercise three days a week.

however, are entering puberty today at younger ages than they did 100 years ago. In the middle of the 1800s, the average girl did not begin to mature until she was at least fourteen. Some people think one reason is that we put hormones in the milk we drink, some of the meat we eat, and some cosmetics and other products we use. Scientists have not been able to prove this, however.

Whatever the age your timer is set for, once puberty starts, it progresses in pretty much the same way for every boy and every girl.

chapter two

HOW DO BOYS' BODIES CHANGE DURING PUBERTY?

Puberty transforms every part of your body, from the top of your head to the bottom of your feet. Inside and out, puberty affects it all. You go into this period of your life as a boy. You come out of it a man.

From start to finish, puberty lasts about six years for most boys. When it is over, the typical adolescent is seventeen or eighteen years old, 4 to 12 inches (10 to 30 cm) taller, 15 to 65 pounds (7 to 29 kilograms) heavier, stronger and more coordinated, and able to reproduce. For this transformation from boyhood to manhood to happen, many changes must take place.

Sex Organs Enlarge

The first noticeable change is that a boy's sex organs get bigger. These organs are the parts of the body that make

The major male sex organs, the penis and the testes, are external. That is, they are on the outside of the body.

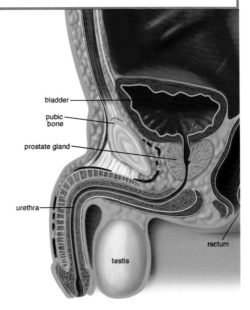

an adult male an adult male. They are the parts that enable males to reproduce. The sex organs are the penis and the testes. The testes, also called testicles, are located in the scrotum. This is a pouch of thin, wrinkled skin underneath the penis. The testes have two purposes. They produce sperm, which unites with a woman's egg to form a baby. They also produce testosterone, the hormone responsible for many of the male's secondary sex characteristics.

Puberty starts when the hypothalamus signals the pituitary gland to release a certain hormone into the bloodstream. The hormone makes its way to the testes, telling them it is time to make testosterone. The testosterone, a steroid hormone, travels through the blood all over the body.

The first change the testosterone makes is in the testes them-selves. The testes start to grow, which means the scrotum has to enlarge, too. Before puberty, the testes measure less than 1 inch (2.5 cm) in length. They are about the size they have been since age one. Once puberty starts, they grow gradually over the next six or so years, until they are about 2 inches (5 cm) long.

As the testes grow, they produce more and more testosterone. A few months after the testes start to enlarge, you can see the effect of the higher hormone level on the penis. Since about age four, most boys' penises are about 1.5 inches (4 cm) long. During puberty, they get bigger and longer. They keep growing for about two years. There is no standard size for an adult penis. The average is between 3 and 6 inches (8 and 15 cm). The size of the penis does not make a person more or less manly than someone else. Like noses and ears, big ones and small ones work equally well.

Hair Grows in New Places

Soon after the sex organs begin to enlarge, you will notice hair growing in the pubic region. This is the area just above and around your penis. Because the sex organs grow slowly, you might not notice that they are getting bigger, so pubic hair may be the first obvious sign that you have entered puberty. For a while, you may have only a few hairs. Over the next six months to a year, much more will appear until it fills in a large triangle in the pubic area. It will become darker, longer, coarser, and thicker. About two years after the first pubic hair sprouts, hair will start to grow under your arms and on your face. It will also grow on your legs. Hair may spread from your pubic region up your abdomen. You might grow hair on your chest and even on your back. Patterns of facial and chest hair are different for different people.

The Body Grows

Among the most dramatic changes of puberty are growth spurts. A spurt is a sudden surge in height, and you can grow very quickly during this period, as much as 4 inches (10 cm) in one year! The biggest spurt, or when you grow the fastest, occurs about two years into puberty, usually between ages thirteen and fifteen. Boys grow at a slower rate than girls, but they grow for a longer period of time. That is why men are generally taller than women. By the time you are eighteen, you are about as tall as you are going to get. You will probably not grow more than three-quarters of an inch (2 cm) after that.

Your bones do not get longer all at once. The first to expand are the ones in your hands and feet. You may outgrow several shoe sizes in one year! Next, the bones in your arms and legs get longer. Finally, the rest of your body grows. This uneven growth can make you feel awkward and clumsy. You might actually trip over your own feet because you are not used to them being so big. Just wait: everything else will eventually catch up.

Because you are growing so rapidly, you may experience growing pains. These are very real aches, usually in the legs. Along with your bones, your muscles are growing and stretching. When you are very active, as you might be when playing a sport, you put extra stress on muscles that are already stressed by the process of growing. Growing pains are normal, and they go away with time. About half of all boys feel some tenderness and swelling around the nipples on their chests. This, too, is normal. It will also go away with time.

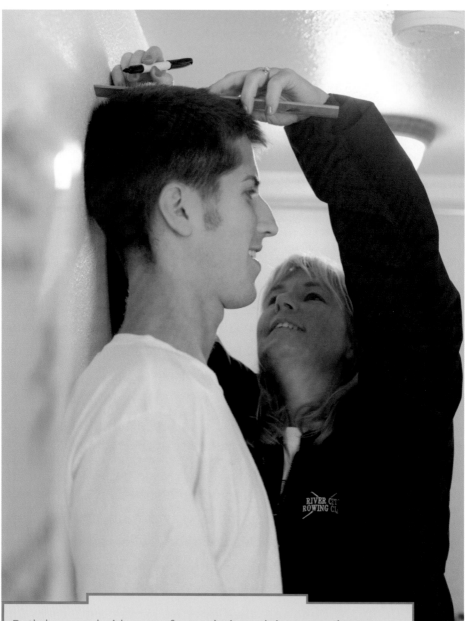

Both boys and girls grow faster during adolescence than at any time except the first year of life. Your growth in this short time will account for 15 to 20 percent of your total height.

Body Shape Changes

In addition to a growth spurt, puberty involves a "strength spurt." Of the 15 to 65 pounds (7 to 30 kg) boys gain during adolescence, most is muscle weight. Boys' muscles nearly double in size during this time. Muscle makes up 50 percent of the average adult male's weight, and fat makes up 15 percent of his weight. By contrast, 40 percent of the average woman's weight is muscle, and 27 percent is fat. The bigger muscles make men stronger than women. The muscles grow after the bones, so the strength spurt occurs after the first year or two of puberty. Often, the muscle growth continues beyond puberty.

As boys' bones and muscles grow, their shoulders move farther apart. Because they have fairly little fat, their hips do not get big. They develop the distinctly male body shape. It is triangular: wide shoulders and narrow hips.

Voice Changes

As your body matures, so do your internal organs. Sometimes called the voice box, the larynx is a muscular organ in your throat. The entire larynx gets longer during puberty. It is made of several pieces of cartilage, which is like soft bone. (Your ears and nose are made of cartilage, too.) As the larynx grows, two pieces of cartilage in the front of the throat come together. This forms the Adam's apple, a lump you can see in men's necks.

Across the larynx lie the vocal cords, two elastic tissues that look a little like rubber bands. When they vibrate, they produce

The Adam's apple gets its name from a Bible story. The first man, Adam, took a bite from an apple, which he had been forbidden to eat, and it got stuck in his throat.

sound, just as the strings of a guitar do. As a boy's larynx grows, his vocal cords become longer and thicker. They loosen a little, making his voice deeper. While this is happening, the voice may crack and break, starting out low and suddenly becoming high in the same sentence—or even the same word! Like all the other developments of puberty, this one takes time. Your voice will eventually settle into an adult sound.

Skin Changes

The same hormones that trigger all of this growth also affect your skin. More specifically, they affect the glands that produce sebum, a kind of oil your skin needs to keep from being dry. The oil gets to your skin through tiny holes called pores. During puberty, the glands often make too much oil. The excess oil, which can combine with dead skin cells and bacteria, often clogs the pores. The clogs form blackheads, whiteheads, and red pimples. This condition is called acne. It usually forms on the face and can appear on the neck, shoulders, upper back, and chest. Almost everyone develops acne during puberty. In some, it is very mild, just a few pimples. In others, it is more severe. People can have outbreaks of acne long after puberty ends, sometimes into their thirties.

The oil glands on your head are also active during puberty. Your hair, just like your face, is oilier at this time. With oily hair may come dandruff, or white flakes of dead skin that fall from your scalp. Shampooing often, even daily, usually takes care of the problem. If you shampoo every day and still have dandruff, you might want to use a medicated shampoo.

Another product you probably want to purchase is deodorant. The hormones of puberty cause you to sweat under your arms. This sweat helps to create an unpleasant odor. Deodorants usually make this less of a problem.

Erections and Wet Dreams

Boys have another potential source of embarrassment during puberty: the spontaneous erection. An erection happens when the penis swells, gets stiff, and stands up. It happens when you are sexually excited, when your penis is rubbed, or sometimes for no apparent reason at all. A spontaneous erection is an erection that occurs suddenly, when you are not expecting it. Even when you were younger, you probably had some erections. During puberty, you are likely to have them more often.

SAM'S STORY

Sam was an average guy. He was average height and had average looks. His grades were average, mostly Cs. Nothing about his appearance or actions made him stand out. That was fine with Sam. A shy boy, he was happy to blend into the crowd.

In ninth grade, however, blending in became harder. For one thing, Sam had somehow become one of the shorter boys in his class. Even his sister, who was a year younger, was taller than he was. Sam also became clumsy. He was always bumping his knees on his desk or knocking things off it. He felt like everyone was looking at him and laughing.

PE was the worst. He was such a klutz and so uncoordinated. He couldn't dribble a basketball. If he even hit a baseball, it never went past the pitcher. Everyone said he threw like a girl.

But Sam had a talent his classmates didn't know about. A very good friend of his helped him get up the nerve to let people see his talent. His school was putting on a play, the musical *Peter Pan*. Anyone could try out. The teacher in charge was a little surprised to see quiet, little Sam brave the auditions. When she heard him sing, she knew why. When she saw him act, she was even more impressed.

Sam would never be a champion football player, but he was the star of the school production. He stood out from his peers in a good way. From then on, whenever they wanted to jam, he was right in the middle of the action. He still thought that everyone was looking at him, but now, he felt, they seemed to like what they saw.

About a year after your penis starts to grow, the testes produce semen. Semen is sperm mixed with other fluids. After you have an erection, the penis can fill with semen and squirt it out. This is called an ejaculation. When an ejaculation takes place while you are asleep, it is called a wet dream. Spontaneous erections and wet dreams are a normal part of adolescence. They happen less often after puberty.

HOW DO GIRLS' BODIES CHANGE DURING PUBERTY?

The transition from girl to woman is more complex than the change from boy to man. When girls become women, their bodies are ready for the awesome task of nurturing and giving birth to children. This requires many changes. The physical changes you can see begin with changes you cannot see. First, your sex organs get bigger just as a boy's do. The reason you do not see them is that boys' sex organs are external, but girls' are internal. They include the ovaries and the uterus. As they enlarge, the ovaries begin to produce estrogen and progesterone, the female hormones responsible for many of the changes in puberty.

Breasts Develop

The first outward sign that a girl has entered puberty is usually breast development. Every girl's breasts develop in the same pattern. As a child, your breasts are flat. When puberty starts, the areola—the dark circle around the nipple—gets wider. The nipple and areola swell a little. This is called breast budding. Just as a flower begins with a small bud that slowly grows and opens, breast development starts as a small mound under your nipple.

In the next six to twelve months, tissue and fat in the breasts begin to multiply. This makes the breasts swell even more. The areolae get darker. At this stage, you might notice that one breast develops before the other, or that the two are not the same size. This is normal, and they usually even out within a few years. Just as your feet are not necessarily the exact same size, one breast may always be a little larger than the other. The difference is generally not very noticeable.

It takes another twelve months or so for the breasts to continue to grow. They do not yet have their adult shape; the nipples and areolae stand out a little from the rest of the breast. Eventually, they develop their soft, rounded shape. That shape comes from milk glands, breast tissue, and fat inside the breasts. All women have about the same amount of milk glands and breast tissue. Whether your breasts are large or small depends on how much fat you have. Full breast development takes two to three years.

Hair Grows in New Places

In some girls, the first indication that puberty has begun is the appearance of hair in the pubic area, the area between the legs. For most, however, pubic hair begins to grow about six months after breasts bud. At first, there are just a few hairs. But within a year, coarse, dark, curly hair fills a triangle shape in the pubic region.

A year or more after pubic hair starts to grow, hair begins to appear under the arms. The hair on girls' legs and arms gets thicker. Sometimes, hair also grows on the upper lip and in front of the ears.

The Body Grows

Around the same time that your breasts start to develop, you will have a growth spurt. As with boys, your hands and feet grow first, then your arms and legs. For probably a year, your legs will seem unusually long. Eventually, the rest of your body grows, too.

It may look as though you shoot up overnight. Actually, you grow about 3 inches (8 cm) in the first year. Then you pick up the pace, growing faster in the next year or so. The rate of growth slows down, but you keep getting taller until you start having menstrual periods. You will probably not grow more than 2 inches (5 cm) after your first period.

During your growth spurt, your bones grow first, and the muscles that are attached to them grow next. When the bones are growing extra quickly, the muscles are stretched tight until their growth catches up. The stretching can hurt, and this is what we call growing pains. If you have them, you usually feel them in your legs. Not everyone gets them, but they are normal and they go away when your growth slows down.

Body Shape Changes

Your bones are not the only part of you that grows during puberty. You also gain weight. Some of that weight gain is muscle, but more of it is fat. In an average, healthy woman, 27 percent of body weight is fat. Most of the new fat is located in the breasts, hips, stomach, and thighs. Fat is what gives women their curvy shape, and it functions to ensure that a fetus will have enough nutrients during a pregnancy.

The curvy shape also comes from an internal growth. Remember the first change of puberty? The ovaries and uterus enlarge. To make room for these growing organs, the bones of the pelvis—the hip bones—move farther apart. The extra room is needed for the time when the mature uterus might hold a growing baby. The hip bones need to be far enough apart for the baby to squeeze through to the outside world.

Menstruation Begins

Preparing your body to have a baby is one of the reasons for the changes of puberty. But your body is able to have a baby long before you might be ready to take care of one. Even if you do decide to have a baby, you probably don't want to have one right after another. How does your body keep itself ready? That is what menstruation is all about. You start to menstruate—have your first period—two to three years after your breasts begin to develop. Breast budding is the first sign of puberty; menstruation is the last.

Talking with your friends can reassure you that what is happening to you is normal. Being a good friend can also make your emotional development healthy.

Changes take place in the female sex organs during puberty. The vagina and uterus become longer. The ovaries enlarge, and the egg cells inside them start to grow.

Before menstruation, your pituitary gland sends new signals to your ovaries and uterus. You have two ovaries, and each one contains about 200,000 eggs. They were already there when you were born, but like the ovaries themselves, they were small and undeveloped. During puberty, they begin to mature. The

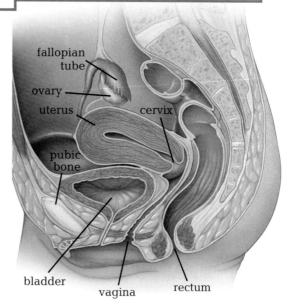

fallopian tube
ovary
uterus
pubic bone
cervix
bladder
vagina
rectum

hormones that go to your ovaries tell them to release an egg; this is called ovulation. If the egg is fertilized by sperm from a male, it will become a baby. The hormones that go to the uterus tell it to get ready in case that egg is fertilized.

The uterus gets ready by preparing a nest with everything the baby will need to grow and thrive. The walls of the uterus thicken with new tissue. The tissue contains blood and other matter that will nourish the fetus in its early stages. When the egg arrives in the uterus, one of two things happens. If the egg is fertilized, it attaches itself to the cushiony lining of the uterus. If it is not fertilized, it does not attach and it dies. In that case, the extra tissue is not needed and the body releases it. It flows out through the vagina. The discharge contains tissue and blood. After the bleeding, the body begins the process again, making a fresh home for a new egg.

The process is the menstrual cycle, and the average cycle is about a month long. The bleeding, which is your period, marks the beginning of the cycle. It usually lasts three to five days. When you first get your period, your cycle will probably not be very regular. It may take twenty-four days one month and thirty the next. You might skip a month or have two periods very close together. Within a year or two, most girls settle into a fairly regular pattern.

Having a period every month may be a nuisance, but it doesn't usually cause major problems. Some girls have cramps, and others have stomach bloating. Some bleed longer than five days, and others bleed a little between periods. You may bleed a lot. You may bleed a little. You may have very irregular periods. All of these situations can be normal. If you have any questions or concerns about your period, just ask your doctor.

Acne and Other Developments

The female hormones of puberty will have some of the same effects on you as the male hormones do on boys. You will develop acne, oily skin and hair, and underarm perspiration and odor. Unlike boys, however, the level of hormones in your body goes up and down somewhat depending on your menstrual cycle. You may notice that acne will flare up just before your period.

Most girls are physically adults by the time they enter high school. Most, however, are not yet emotionally or socially mature, and few are ready for adult responsibilities.

The average girl in the United States has had her first period by age thirteen. By then, she is almost as tall as she will get, she has an adult body shape, and her ovaries are producing eggs. Physically, at least, she is fully a woman.

DO EMOTIONS CHANGE, TOO?

Puberty involves the way you feel and the way you look. It is a time of great physical change, and our emotions are partly biological. The hormones that cause such drastic changes in our physical bodies affect our emotions, too. Just as the physical developments of early adolescence can appear sudden and dramatic, the emotions are often surprising and extreme as well.

Sexual Appetite

The hormones released during puberty can create an interest in the opposite sex. Boys and girls will soon think about what it would be like to have sex. The attraction is not just emotional; it is also biological. Without it, people might never get married and have children. The desire to be sexually intimate is called a sexual appetite because it becomes a craving, just like the hunger for food.

Just like the yearning for food, sexual appetite is something you can control. Think of someone preparing a delicious dinner for you from the very finest ingredients. You might not eat all day so you can relish the wonderful feast when it is time. You control yourself, passing up junk food and even good food so you can enjoy the best. That is what it is like to wait to have sex. You pass up short-term, immediate pleasure—as well as the very real possibility of premature pregnancy, diseases, and heartaches—for long-term happiness.

Strong and Wild

During puberty, feelings are often exaggerated. Everything that happens seems bigger to you than to the adults in your life. Things that don't bother others may seem impossible for you.

Something that is upsetting may feel like the end of the world. Something happy may put you on cloud nine for days. Every emotion is intense. Fear, joy, disappointment, irritation— every feeling seems larger than life.

You might find yourself sobbing over a very small hurt. Or you might blow up over a tiny offense. You might suddenly feel happy or sad for no apparent reason. Your mood might go in a matter of moments from being pleasant and agreeable to being silent and sulky. You—or those around you—may feel like you are on a roller coaster: up one minute and down the next. Strong emotions and mood swings are normal during this time. Your hormone levels will eventually calm down, and so will the intensity of your feelings.

> The many changes that happen so quickly during puberty can be confusing and frustrating. These feelings, coupled with a desire for independence, often turn into anger, which is a normal feeling.

All About Me

One of the most common feelings of early adolescence is fear or worry. With so many changes happening so quickly, you may worry if you are normal. How will all the changes turn out? What will you look like and be like as an adult? Do others notice the things about you that seem different? Will something you cannot control embarrass you? Will people accept you?

Because so many changes are occurring, it is easy to forget that your friends and classmates are all in the same boat. Most teens are focused very much on themselves. They have what psychologists say is an "imaginary audience." That is, they think everyone is looking at them. The truth is, your classmates are probably too concerned about themselves to notice you.

Still, your fear of what others are thinking about you leads to a strong challenge at this time: peer pressure. One way that people handle peer pressure is to try to be like everyone else. They wear the same clothes, talk the same way, and assume

The number-one reason young people experiment with smoking, drinking, or drugs is that their peers ask them to try them. That's why it's important for teens to choose their friends carefully.

the same attitudes. This is not bad when your peers—friends who are your age—make good choices. But if they make choices that are harmful, you can be tempted to follow along. You might even choose to do something you really don't want to, just so others will not make fun of you. Peer pressure can be hard to resist, so make sure your peers are people you want to be like.

Your Brain Changes

To function properly in the adult world, you must think in adult ways. These reasoning skills begin to develop during puberty.

While your bones and organs are undergoing a growth spurt, so is your brain. The part of your brain that has to do with thinking, self-control, planning, and reasoning is maturing. New brain cells are forming, and ones that are not used are dying. This process continues until about your twenties.

The fact that teenagers' brains are still forming may explain some of the illogical behavior of many young people. Their thinking is often not rational. Some take risks that could cause great harm: drinking, smoking, taking drugs, having sex, doing daredevil stunts. They act as though they are invincible—nothing bad can ever happen to them. Teens may not have the reasoning ability to make the wisest choices, but that does not mean they must choose destructive behaviors. They can follow the advice of trustworthy adults, even if it doesn't make sense to them at the time.

Search for Identity

Part of growing up is discovering who you are. As a child, you probably did not think much about what is important in life, what you believe, and what you want to do as an adult. You probably accepted what your parents or other adults said about these matters. Yet your beliefs will guide your decisions when you are older.

In addition, you will need to figure out where and how you fit in with other people. Are you a leader or a follower? A dreamer or a careful planner? A businessperson or an artist? Do you create new things or make old things better? Do you prefer physical or mental exercise? Calm surroundings or lots of activity? Which is more important to you: knowing lots of people or having a few

Myths and Facts
About Puberty

 Eating greasy foods such as french fries makes acne worse. Fact ➤ Acne is caused by oil production inside your body, so nothing you eat makes any difference.

 Exposing skin to the sun will clear up acne. Fact ➤ Tanning will darken the skin, which makes the acne less noticeable, but it does nothing to take it away.

Popping and squeezing a blackhead makes it disappear faster. Fact ➤ Popping a blackhead or a pimple can cause it to get infected or inflamed, making it worse. Doing that can even leave a scar.

 Shaving makes hair grow back thicker. Fact ➤ Shaving cuts hair at the skin's surface, and hair grows from beneath the surface. When hair grows back after shaving, it is short. A patch of shorter hairs can look thicker than the same number of longer hairs.

Taking advantage of opportunities to learn new things and participate in a variety of positive activities will help you decide who you are and who you want to be.

close friends? Winning or doing a good job? You are a unique person, different from anyone in your family, different from all your friends. During adolescence, you will work at finding out exactly who you are.

In the search for your identity, you may try new things. Some you will like, and others you won't. You might try cigarettes, for example, and decide that you will not be a smoker. Searches are often processes of trial and error. You will look for role models, people to imitate. You will probably examine people very closely, seeing if you like their ideas and actions. You may find that your parents do not always agree with your teachers, and your friends do not agree with one another. All of these different ideas can be confusing. You will try to figure out which ones you will believe for yourself. Don't get discouraged. Determining your identity is a lifelong process. It begins in adolescence.

Desire for Independence

Another important process that begins in adolescence is the movement toward independence. All your life you have been growing away from your parents. When you were a baby, you were totally dependent on them. As you aged, you were gradually given more control over your own life. You were allowed to choose what clothes you wanted to wear or whether you wanted to go to a particular place. You probably wanted to make more of those decisions. And as you mature physically, as your mental abilities become sharper, and as you start to think about your identity, you will seek even more independence. This is good because you will soon be completely independent of the adults in your life.

Making many of those choices is a privilege, and with every privilege comes a responsibility. When you are an adult, you will have major control over your own life and possibly the lives of others. Now is the time to learn to handle responsibility. This means taking the blame—or the praise—for the consequences of your decisions and actions. It means figuring out what needs to

Driving a car is a big step toward independence. This privilege carries with it many responsibilities: knowing the laws, learning to drive well, buying gas and insurance, and even keeping the vehicle clean.

be done and doing it. It means if something you do turns out badly, you fix it.

Your desire for independence can create conflict with your parents. You may want more freedom and fewer responsibilities than they want to give you. Try to remember that in the adult world, opportunities and obligations should be balanced. The more responsibility you are willing to take, the more privileges you can enjoy. Believe it or not, your parents want you to be independent . . . when you are ready. That is what puberty is about: the beginning of the changes that prepare you for your adult life.

five

HOW SHOULD I HANDLE ALL THESE CHANGES?

During puberty, your body changes more in a shorter period than in almost any other time in your life. This can be stressful, both physically and emotionally. The best way to ease the stress is to practice the basic habits of good health.

Good, Healthy Habits

A healthful diet will give your body the nutrients it needs for the many changes it is making. The best diet contains a variety of foods, including grains, protein, vegetables, and fruits. Don't eat too many fats and sugars. Your growing bones need calcium, so drink milk and eat dairy products such as yogurt and cheese. Both boys and girls need iron, but girls need extra because they lose iron during their monthly periods.

Physical exercise is also important for good overall health. Not only can it make you feel better, but it can also

How much you exercise during your teen years will make a huge difference later. The more you exercise, the more your bones build. After adolescence, you lose a little bit of bone every year.

strengthen your bones as they grow. If you have menstrual cramps or other pains, exercising can ease the discomfort. But keep it reasonable. Extreme exercising can make muscles ache and prevent periods from occurring. In extreme cases, it is an addiction that is linked to eating disorders.

Many young teens, especially boys, are interested in bulking up or toning their maturing muscles. They wonder if exercising, particularly weight lifting, will help or hurt their bone growth and muscle development. In general, moderate exercise is good, and overdoing it is bad. If weights are too heavy, lifting them can injure the bones and keep them from growing. The key to strengthening your muscles is not how much you lift, but how often you lift. Fifteen repetitions in one session is a great start. You want to build up your bones and muscles a little at a time.

You may be surprised to find that you are tired. All that growing is physically demanding. You need more sleep now than when you were a young child. During puberty, your body requires ten hours of sleep for maximum health.

What Can I Do About Growing Pains?

Growing pains are aches you can feel in your legs as your muscles are stretching to catch up with your growing bones. They are actually muscle spasms. When you feel this pain, stretch your feet and toes. Massage the tender spots slowly. If the pain continues, apply moist heat over the areas. If you get growing pains often, you might want to do stretching exercises daily. These will relax the muscles and possibly prevent the pain.

Ten Great Questions to Ask Your School Nurse

1 (Male): My chest hurts, and it looks like I'm getting breasts. Is something wrong?

2 (Female): One breast is growing, and the other is not. Is something wrong?

3 (Male): My penis is still very small. Is it going to grow more?

4 (Female): I get very bad cramps with my period. Is something wrong? What can I do to make it hurt less?

5 Should I use a special soap for my acne?

6 How can I protect my private parts during sports?

7 Can I do strength-training exercises?

8 My legs hurt at night. What can I do about that?

9 I am gaining a lot of weight. Is it OK to go on a diet?

10 Should I eat certain foods while my body is growing?

What Can I Do About Acne?

There is little you can do to stop acne. Because it is caused by hormones and not by eating oily foods, you cannot control it with diet. You can make it less severe, however, by keeping your face and other areas clean. The less dirt and oil on your skin, the less chance of clogging pores. You do not need to wash your face more than twice a day unless you have been sweating or if your dermatologist recommends it. Sweat can clog pores. Wash gently; scrubbing hard can irritate the skin and make matters worse. You do not need special soap.

Do not put anything oily on your face that could clog pores more. Some makeup products have oil in them, and so do certain types of sunscreen. Oil-free makeup is your best bet, but be sure to remove it completely at night. Your hands have natural oils on them, so try not to touch your face. Your hair will be oilier, too, so keep it off your face, neck, and back. Consider not wearing a hat. Hats can block pores, and acne often appears where a hatband has been.

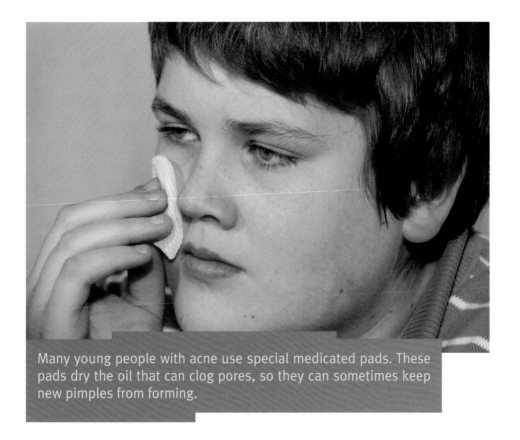

Many young people with acne use special medicated pads. These pads dry the oil that can clog pores, so they can sometimes keep new pimples from forming.

You can buy creams and lotions that make breakouts less severe. Look for products that contain benzoyl peroxide or salicylic acid. Benzoyl peroxide kills the bacteria that help create acne. Salicylic acid dries the skin. If your acne is severe, a doctor can give you stronger creams or medicines that can keep pimples from forming or get rid of them quickly.

Whatever you do, do not pop or squeeze any blackhead, whitehead, or pimple! This may release some of the oil, but it can also make the area infected or inflamed. Even worse, the popped area usually forms a pitlike scar.

When Would I Need to See a Doctor?

Every teenager wonders if he or she is normal. The answer is usually yes! But if something is really bothering you, talk to someone about it. Remember, there is a wide range of what is normal. People in the same family, even twins, often experience the changes of puberty at different rates. Talk to your parents or another trustworthy adult. If you are still concerned, see a doctor.

If you see signs of puberty before age eight if you're a girl, and age nine if you're a boy, you may want to see a doctor. Early puberty is normal for some people, but starting so young can cause problems later on. People who start puberty early usually finish it more quickly than others. That means their bones do not have as long a time to grow. They can end up as very short adults. Doctors can give medications that stop the hormones from doing their work. Later, you stop taking the medications, and puberty gets back on a more typical schedule.

If you are around fifteen and have not seen breast budding or development of the testes, you should talk with your doctor. Late puberty can keep your bones from building, and thinner bones break more easily. Doctors can give you hormones that will get you started. Another cause for concern is if you see signs that puberty has begun but then the process seems interrupted. If a girl has begun to develop but has not had a period within five years, she should seek medical attention. The same goes for a boy who has started puberty but whose penis has not grown to its adult length within five years.

Adolescence can feel like an emotional roller coaster. Sharing your feelings with friends can make the highs higher and the lows not so low. (A parent can be one of those friends!)

How Do I Handle the Emotional Ups and Downs?

Everyone experiences intense emotions some of the time, but those going through puberty have strong emotions most of the time. Your emotional state is affected by your overall health. When you are bothered by mood swings, go back to the basics. Make sure you are eating right, exercising, and getting enough rest. Avoid situations that stress you out. When you feel particularly stressed, try exercising. Physical activity relieves stress and releases calming chemicals in your brain.

Remind yourself that no feeling will last forever. If you feel intensely sad or angry, hold on. Before long you will feel happy or calm again. No matter how strong the emotion, it will eventually fade. That's just how your hormones work at this time. In rare cases, teens experience depression that does not let up. If you feel extremely sad for many days at a time, your hormones may need to be better balanced. A doctor can give you medications that will do this.

You may not be able to control how you feel, but you can control how you act. Think about how the people around you would feel if you unleash your anger or frustration on them. Controlling outbursts of emotion will make you more pleasant to be around. Get in the habit of stopping, taking a breath, and waiting before you speak and act. Try to put things in perspective. Is what you are upset about really as important as it feels? Learning to control your reactions will make you a stronger, nicer person.

How Do I Handle Peer Pressure?

The desire to fit in with your peers is a normal part of adolescence. The way to make it positive is to choose responsible peers. If the people you hang with have good values, chances are they will influence you in good ways. Find at least one friend who will stick with you in making the right choices. It is easier to resist negative peer pressure when you are not alone.

Peers are your classmates, neighbors, or cousins. You may not be able to choose your peers, but you can choose how much you want to be like them.

Peer pressure does not really come from your peers. It comes from pressure inside you to want to fit in. Think of trying to crush two soda cans, one empty and one full. The empty one crumples easily because the pressure on the outside is greater than what is inside. But the full one resists the pressure to bend because there is more strength inside than outside. The best way to stand strong in the midst of any pressure is to build yourself up. Explore your talents. Do well in school. Help other people. Be kind and strong. The more pleased you are with who you are and what you do, the better equipped you will be to handle all the challenges of puberty.

acne A skin condition in which the pores become clogged, resulting in whiteheads, blackheads, and pimples.

Adam's apple Lump at the front of an adult male's neck formed as the larynx grows during puberty.

adolescence Period of time between childhood and adulthood that begins with puberty.

blackhead A plug made of sebum, bacteria, and dead skin cells that forms in a pore of the skin. The plug appears as a pinhead-sized black spot.

delayed puberty The condition in which the physical transformation from childhood to adulthood begins later than normal, after age sixteen for girls and age fourteen for boys.

erection The action of the penis swelling, stiffening, and standing up. An erection is usually caused by sexual stimulation.

estrogen One of the female hormones produced in the ovaries.

hormone A chemical produced in one organ that travels to another organ to stimulate it to begin or stop a function.

hypothalamus A gland in the brain that controls, among other things, when many other glands release their hormones.

larynx Organ in the throat that contains the vocal cords.

organ A bodily part that has a particular function.

ovaries Female sex organs that produce hormones and eggs.

period Monthly, bloody discharge of the wall of the uterus.

pituitary gland The gland that produces many of the hormones that cause puberty.

precocious puberty The condition in which the physical transformation from childhood to adulthood begins earlier than normal, before age eight for girls and age nine for boys.

primary sex characteristics The physical traits that distinguish males from females: the male penis and related organs and the female vagina and related organs.

progesterone One of the female hormones produced in the ovaries.

pubic Referring to the region between the legs around the pelvic bones.

scrotum The pouch in males that contains the testes.

sebum Oily substance produced by glands beneath the skin.

secondary sex characteristics The physical traits that, in addition to the primary sex characteristics, distinguish adult males from adult females: body shape, facial and body hair, and percentages of fat and muscle.

testes The organs located in the scrotum of males that produce testosterone and sperm. Also called testicles.

testosterone A male hormone produced in the testes. A small amount is also present in females.

uterus The organ in the female body where a fertilized egg grows into a baby.

vagina The canal that extends from the lower end of the uterus to the outside of the female body.

whitehead A plug made of sebum, bacteria, and dead skin cells that forms in a pore of the skin. The plug appears as a raised white spot.

Family Doctor
Web site of the American Academy of Family Physicians
Web site: http://familydoctor.org
This Web site has easy-to-find information on health
topics for teens.

HealthFinder
P.O. Box 1133
Washington, DC 20013
E-mail: healthfinder@nhic.org
Web site: http://www.healthfinder.gov
This library provides health information for teens.

Teen Growth
11274 W. Hillsborough Avenue
Tampa, FL 33635
E-mail: feedback@teengrowth.com
Web site: http://www.teengrowth.com
This organization has information on all kinds of teen-
related topics.

Teen Health Web Site of the Nemours Foundation
Web site: http://kidshealth.org
This Web site has easy-to-find and easy-to-understand
discussions on health topics of interest to teens.

Women's College Hospital of the Canadian Health Network
790 Bay Street, Suites 902–908
Toronto, ON M5G 1N8
E-mail: info@womenshealthmatters.ca
Web site: http://www.womenshealthmatters.ca
  This Web site has up-to-date news and information on
  women's health, diseases, and lifestyle trends.

Hot Lines

Teenage Health Resource Line of the Lucile Packard Children's
Hospital at Stanford University
725 Welch Road
Palo Alto, CA 94304
(888) 711-TEEN (8336), weekdays 12–8 PM; weekends 8 AM to 8 PM
Web site: http://www.lpch.org/ForPatientsVisitors/
  PatientServices/TeenLine/TeenHealthLine.html
  This hotline provides anonymous and confidential answers
  to health-related questions from nurses.

Teen Health Web Site and Hotline
Nova Scotia, Canada
(800) 420-8336
Web site: http://www.chebucto.ns.ca/Health/TeenHealth
  This organization is dedicated to providing access on health
  and medical information to the public.

Web Sites

Due to the changing nature of Internet links, Rosen Publishing
has developed an online list of Web sites related to the subject
of this book. This site is updated regularly. Please use this link
to access the list:

http://www.rosenlinks.com/faq/pube

For Further Reading

Bailey, Jacqui. *Sex, Puberty, and All That Stuff: A Guide to Growing Up*. Hauppauge, NY: Barrons, 2004.

Basso, Michael J. *The Underground Guide to Teenage Sexuality*. Minneapolis, MN: Fairview Press, 2003.

Bell, Ruth. *Changing Bodies, Changing Lives: A Book for Teens on Sex and Relationships*. New York, NY: Three Rivers Press, 1998.

Bryan, Jenny. *Adolescence*. Chicago, IL: Raintree, 2000.

Crump, Marguerite. *Don't Sweat It! Everybody's Answers to Questions You Don't Want to Ask: A Guide for Young People*. Minneapolis, MN: Free Spirit, 2002.

Dobson, James. *Preparing for Adolescence: How to Survive the Coming Years of Change*. Ventura, CA: Regal, 1978.

Elliot-Wright, Susan. *Puberty*. Chicago, IL: Raintree, 2003.

Favor, Lesli J. *Everything You Need to Know About Growth Spurts and Delayed Growth*. New York, NY: Rosen Publishing, 2002.

Fiscus, James W. *Coping with Growth Spurts and Delayed Growth*. New York, NY: Rosen Publishing, 2002.

Gravelle, Karen. *What's Going on Down There? Answers to Questions Boys Find Hard to Ask*. New York, NY: Walker and Company, 1998.

Guest, Elissa Haden. *Girl Stuff: A Survival Guide to Growing Up*. New York, NY: Harcourt, 2000.

Harris, Robie H. *It's Perfectly Normal: Changing Bodies, Growing Up, Sex, and Sexual Health.* Cambridge, MA: Candlewick Press, 1994.

Madaras, Lynda. *The "What's Happening to My Body?" Book for Boys: A Growing-Up Guide for Preteens and Teens.* New York, NY: Newmarket Press, 2000.

Madaras, Lynda. *The "What's Happening to My Body?" Book for Girls: A Growing-Up Guide for Preteens and Teens.* New York, NY: Newmarket Press, 2000.

Pascoe, Elaine. *Teen Dreams: The Journey Through Puberty.* Farmington Hills, MI: Thomas Gale, 2004.

Silverstein, Alvin, Virginia B. Silverstein, and Laura Silverstein Nunn. *Puberty.* New York, NY: Scholastic, 2000.

Silverthorne, Sandy. *Surviving Zits: How to Cope with Your Changing Self.* Cincinnati, OH: Standard, 2004.

Bibliography

Christensen, Barbara Lauritsen, and Elaine Oden Kockrow, eds. *Foundations of Nursing*. 3rd ed. New York, NY: Mosby, 1999.

Clayman, Charles B., ed. *American Medical Association Home Medical Encyclopedia*. New York, NY: Random House, 1989.

Encyclopaedia Britannica. "Puberty." Retrieved May 25, 2006 (http://search.eb.com/eb/article-9061786?query=puberty&ct=eb).

National Institute of Mental Health. "Teenage Brain: A Work in Progress." National Institutes of Health Publication No. 01-4929. 2001. Retrieved May 25, 2006 (http://www.nimh.nih.gov/Publicat/teenbrain.cfm).

Nethersole, Shari. "Kids and Weight Lifting." Family Education Network. Retrieved May 2, 2006 (http://life.familyeducation.com/sports/safety/42241.html).

Thomas, Clayton L., ed. *Taber's Cyclopedic Medical Dictionary*. Philadelphia, PA: F. A. Davis, 1997.

myths and facts about, 39
precocious, 12, 13
and pubic hair, 18, 27–28
and skin, 8, 22–23, 32
ten facts about, 10–11
ten great questions to ask
   about, 47–48
and voice, 8, 21–22
and weight, 8, 10, 13, 16, 21,
   29, 46, 48

S

salicylic acid, 49
scrotum, 17
sebum, 22
secondary sex characteristics, 7,
   8, 17
semen, 25
sexual appetite, 34, 35

sperm, 17, 25, 31

T

testes, 11, 17, 18,
   25, 50
testosterone, 17, 18

U

uterus, 26, 29, 31

V

vagina, 7, 32
vocal cords, 21, 22

W

wet dreams, 25
whiteheads, 23, 49

About the Author

Ann Byers is an educator and writer who lives in Fresno, California. She works with teenage parents and teaches classes on preparing for adolescence for parents and preteens.

Photo Credits

Cover © age fotostock/SuperStock; p. 5 © www.istockphoto.com/James Pauls; p. 7 Emin Kuliyev/Shutterstock.com; p. 9 © L. Birmingham/Custom Medical Stock Photo, Inc.; p. 13 © www.istockphoto.com/Mike Panic; p. 14 (top) © www.istockphoto.com/Duncan Walker; p. 14 (bottom) © www.istockphoto.com/Oscar Williams; p. 17 © B. Wainwright/Custom Medical Stock Photo, Inc.; p. 20 © Jed and Kaoru Share/Corbis; p. 22 © T. Kruesselmann/zefa/Corbis; p. 30 Galina Barskaya/Shutterstock.com; p. 31 © Brian Evans/Photo Researchers, Inc.; p. 33 © Ilya Rabkin/Shutterstock, Inc.; p. 36 Anita Patterson Peppers/Shutterstock.com; p. 37 © www.istockphoto.com/Simone van den Berg; p. 40 Laurence Gough/Shutterstock.com; p. 42 © www.istockphoto.com/Lisa F. Young; p. 45 © www.istockphoto.com/Phil Date; p. 49 © www.istockphoto.com/Anita Patterson; p. 51 © www.istockphoto.com; p. 53 © www.istockphoto.com.

Editor: Jun Lim; Series Designer: Evelyn Horovicz
Photo Researcher: Hillary Arnold